WAR STORIES

ANIMAL HEROES

Jane Bingham

Heinemann
LIBRARY

Chicago, Illinois

www.heinemannraintree.com
Visit our website to find out
more information about
Heinemann-Raintree books.

To order:
☎ Phone 888-454-2279
🖱 Visit www.heinemannraintree.com
to browse our catalog and order online.

Edited by Louise Galpine and Vaarunika Dharmapala
Designed by Clare Webber and Steve Mead
Original illustrations © Capstone Global Library
 Ltd 2011
Illustrated by KJA-Artists.com
Picture research by Elizabeth Alexander
Originated by Capstone Global Library Ltd
Printed and bound in China by Leo Paper
 Products Ltd

15 14 13 12 11
10 9 8 7 6 5 4 3 2 1

**Library of Congress Cataloging-in-Publication
Data**
Bingham, Jane.
 Animal heroes / Jane Bingham. —1st ed.
   p. cm.—(War stories)
 Includes bibliographical references and index.
 ISBN 978-1-4329-4834-4 (hc)—ISBN 978-1-4329-
4842-9 (pb) 1. Working animals—Juvenile literature.
2. Animal heroes—Juvenile literature. I. Title.
 SF170.B56 2011
 355.4'24—dc22   2010029577

Acknowledgments
We would like to thank the following for permission
to reproduce photographs: © Mark R. Lenz p. **23**;
© Nancy J. Cox, Massachusetts p. **10**; Alamy p.
27 (© The Protected Art Archive); Canada. Dept.
of National Defence/Library and Archives Canada/
PA-116791 pp. **18–19**; Corbis pp. **5** (© Peter
MACDIARMID/Reuters), **7** (© Hulton-Deutsch
Collection), **12–13** (© Bettmann), **25** (© Reuters),
26 (© Fabrizio Bensch/Reuters); Getty Images pp. **4**
(Mauricio Lima/AFP), **6** (H. Motte/Mansell/Time Life
Pictures), **15** (Paul Thompson/FPG/Hulton Archive),
16 (Boyer/Roger Viollet), **21** (Fox Photos), **22** (Marco
Di Lauro), **24** (Alexander Joe/AFP); Photograph
courtesy of PDSA p. **18**, p. **20**; Photolibrary pp.
9 (DEA Picture Library), **14**; The Art Archive p. **8**
(Musée du Château de Versailles/Alfredo Dagli Orti);
Shutterstock **background design and features**
(© oriontrail).

Cover photograph of arms and explosives search
dog Treo and his handler, Sergeant Dave Heyhoe,
posing with the PDSA Dickin Medal reproduced with
permission of Getty Images (Carl Court/AFP).

We would like to thank John Allen Williams,
Professor of Political Science, Loyola University,
Chicago, for his invaluable help in the preparation
of this book.

CONTENTS

INTRODUCTION. 4

ANIMALS IN BATTLE 6

ANIMALS IN WORLD WAR I 12

ANIMALS IN WORLD WAR II. 18

ANIMALS IN RECENT WARS. 22

CONCLUSION 26

ANIMAL HEROES AROUND THE WORLD 28

GLOSSARY. 30

FIND OUT MORE. 31

INDEX 32

Words appearing in the text in bold, **like this**, are explained in the glossary.

Look out for these boxes:

WHAT WOULD YOU DO?
Imagine what it would be like to make difficult choices in wartime.

REMEMBERING BRAVERY
Find out about the ways in which we remember courageous acts today.

NUMBER CRUNCHING
Learn the facts and figures about wars and battles.

SECRET HEROES
Find out about the brave individuals who didn't make it into the history books.

When you think of war heroes, do you ever picture horses, dogs, or pigeons? In fact, all kinds of creatures take part in wars. Over the centuries, animals have shown great bravery in war. Many people see these courageous creatures as heroes.

All kinds of heroes

Animals have been used in war for thousands of years. Some have charged into battle with soldiers on their backs. Others have carried important messages or transported loads for hundreds of miles. Some remarkable creatures have helped in rescue operations, and many have risked their lives checking for unexploded bombs.

▲ Sniffer dogs are heroes of modern warfare. They often search for dangerous **explosives**.

SECRET HEROES

During World War I, soldiers sometimes kept glowworms in glass jars. The light sent out by the glowworms allowed the soldiers to read maps at night. It was too faint to be spotted by enemy troops.

Even though animals have no choice about their role in war, they have often acted like heroes. In the face of great hardship and danger, they have been brave, loyal, and determined.

▼ The Animals in War Memorial in London shows horses, donkeys, dogs, elephants, and camels. It even includes some tiny glowworms!

REMEMBERING BRAVERY

The Animals in War **Memorial** in London, England, is dedicated to "all the animals that served and died alongside British and allied forces in wars and campaigns throughout time."

ANIMALS IN BATTLE

In the ancient world, soldiers relied on horses and dogs to help them in battle. Asian warriors started riding horses around 6,000 years ago, and the ancient Egyptians rode in battle **chariots** pulled by horses. The armies of ancient Egypt, Greece, and Rome included dogs. Fighting dogs sometimes wore spiked collars and armor to protect them from attack.

Elephants and pigs

Elephants played an important role in ancient battles. In India, warrior kings rode to war on the backs of enormous war elephants. Persian and Greek commanders trained elephants to charge at their enemies, scattering men and horses in all directions.

▼ This painting shows elephants being used in a battle against the ancient Romans.

The ancient Romans found a way to fight back against elephant charges. They led herds of pigs into battle to face the elephants. When the charge began, the pigs squealed in panic. The elephants were terrified by the sound of the squealing, and they turned and fled from the battlefield.

NUMBER CRUNCHING

In 218 BCE, the military leader Hannibal launched an attack on Rome. He led his army for 2,414 kilometers (1,500 miles) from Carthage, his city in North Africa, to Italy, crossing two mountain ranges on the way. It is believed that Hannibal took 12,000 horses and 37 elephants to war. Only half the horses and just a single elephant survived the long, hard journey.

▶ In the deserts of Arabia in the Middle East, warriors fought on camels. The camels were trained to bite and kick their enemies.

Marvelous Marengo

Throughout the history of warfare, horses and warriors have faced danger together. It is not surprising that some special friendships have developed between soldiers and their battle horses.

The famous French general Napoleon Bonaparte had a favorite horse. The horse was named Marengo, and he managed to stay calm even in the fiercest **conflict**. Napoleon rode Marengo into battle for 15 years. The plucky little horse even survived a 4,828-kilometer (3,000-mile) trek to the Russian city of Moscow and back. He carried his master through snow, hail, and rain.

In 1815 Napoleon was defeated by the British Army at the Battle of Waterloo. Marengo was wounded, but he survived. He was rescued by a British officer who took him back to England. Crowds of sightseers lined the streets of London to see Napoleon's famous horse.

▶ Marengo had to climb steep mountain passes and face terrifying enemy gunfire.

REMEMBERING BRAVERY

In 1876 the U.S. Army was defeated by several different groups of Native Americans at the Battle of Little Bighorn. One of the few survivors on the army's side was the warhorse Comanche. He had been badly wounded in the battle, but he was nursed back to health. Comanche became a symbol of the spirit of survival. He toured the United States until his death. Today, people can still see Comanche on display at the University of Kansas.

▼ Hundreds of horses were wounded and killed at the Battle of Little Bighorn.

Lucky mascots

For centuries, soldiers have kept tame animals known as **mascots**. Military mascots are supposed to bring good luck in battle. They are also pets for the troops. Dogs are very popular mascots, but some armies choose more unusual animals to take to war.

Civil War creatures

Between 1861 and 1865, the American **Civil War** was fought between **Union** troops from the North and **Confederate** troops from the South. Soldiers on both sides had some surprising creatures as their mascots. They included a tame bear, a raccoon, and a badger.

The most famous Civil War mascot was a bald eagle named Old Abe. He had been tamed by Native Americans before being sold to Union troops and becoming their mascot. Old Abe took part in 37 battles. He sat on a perch beside the Union flag and screeched violently at the Confederate troops.

▶ This statue is of Sallie the terrier, who was a Union mascot during the Civil War. After the Battle of Gettysburg in 1863, she stayed with injured Union soldiers. Sallie kept watch for three days without food or water until help arrived.

Even during the fiercest battle, Old Abe stayed on his perch, giving comfort to the Union troops and terrifying the enemy.

Horses, mules, donkeys, dogs, and pigeons all played an active part in World War I (1914–18). At first, mainly European countries were involved in the war. Then, in 1917, the United States joined Great Britain and fought against Germany. Most of the fighting took place in northern France and Belgium, in an area known as the **western front**.

Horses in World War I

Within a few months of the start of the war, the western front had become a sea of mud. Teams of farm horses struggled through the mud, pulling heavy guns, ambulances, and **mobile kitchens**. The horses often sank up to their bellies in mud.

Some horses carried soldiers into battle. These **cavalry** battles ended in disaster, as the horses got stuck in the mud and were easily shot down.

▼ These World War I soldiers have just escaped from an explosion, thanks to their horses.

NUMBER CRUNCHING

At least eight million horses died in World War I.

Horses suffered terribly in World War I. They were easy targets for enemy gunners, and many swallowed **poison gas** and choked to death. The horses were overworked and underfed, and thousands of them died from exhaustion. In spite of all their suffering, the horses showed great patience, steadiness, and courage.

REMEMBERING BRAVERY

In his novel *War Horse*, Michael Morpurgo tells the story of Joey, a farm horse who was sent to serve in World War I. Joey's tragic tale is based on the experience of real war horses. It has been made into a very popular play.

Simpson and his donkey

Some battles in World War I were fought on the coast of Turkey. The fighting was very fierce, and many people were killed or wounded. One Australian soldier decided to use donkeys to carry the wounded to safety.

Jack Simpson and his favorite donkey, known as Duffy, carried injured soldiers away from the battlefield. They climbed down a steep mountain path to reach the hospital base. Simpson and Duffy were constantly under fire, but they kept on working night and day. They carried the wounded for almost a month, until Simpson was shot dead.

▼ This statue of Simpson and Duffy helping a wounded soldier is at the Australian War **Memorial** in Canberra.

Red Cross dogs

At least 10,000 dogs helped the **Red Cross** in their work of caring for the wounded. After a battle, Red Cross dogs were sent out to search for injured men. The dogs were trained to take the cap of a wounded man back to the hospital base. Then they would show the **stretcher-bearers** where to find the man.

SECRET HEROES

Soldiers on the western front sometimes made pets of stray cats. The cats were very useful, because they killed the rats that lived in the **trenches**.

▼ Red Cross dogs carry a first aid kit to be used by soldiers.

Pigeons with cameras

Pigeons played an important part in World War I. Some pigeons worked as spies, flying over enemy land with a camera strapped to their chest. Others carried messages across the battlefields.

A pigeon friend

One of the bravest messenger pigeons was named Cher Ami, which means "dear friend" in French. He was with a group of U.S. soldiers when they became trapped in a deep valley. The soldiers spent a terrible day facing enemy fire. Then some U.S. gunners started to shoot at them, not realizing that they were aiming at friends.

► Spy pigeons flew over enemy lines with automatic cameras. They were easy to spot, and many were shot down.

In a desperate attempt to save his men, the commander wrote a message. He gave his exact position and told the gunners to stop firing. Then he fixed the message to Cher Ami's leg. The pigeon flew for 40 kilometers (25 miles) to deliver the message. As soon as the gunners read the message, they stopped firing. Two hundred men were rescued, thanks to the bravery of Cher Ami.

▲ Cher Ami flew 12 missions before he was badly injured. On his last mission he was wounded in the eye, chest, and leg, but he still managed to deliver his message.

REMEMBERING BRAVERY

After the war, the French government gave Cher Ami a very special medal. The medal was the Croix de Guerre, one of France's highest honors. It is awarded for bravery in war, but it is usually only given to human heroes.

ANIMALS IN WORLD WAR II

World War II lasted from 1939 to 1945. The war was fought to stop the **aggression** of Germany, under **Nazi** Party leader Adolf Hitler, and Japan. There were battles in Europe, Africa, and Asia, and millions of people were killed. Armies in World War II usually relied on tanks rather than horses, but dogs and messenger pigeons had important roles to play.

Gander the hero

One of the animal heroes of World War II was a dog named Gander. He was the **mascot** of a **regiment** of Canadian soldiers. The soldiers were based on the island of Hong Kong, in the Pacific Ocean.

Gander's regiment helped to defend Hong Kong from attack. In one of these attacks, a **hand grenade** was thrown at a group of wounded soldiers. Gander was a clever dog who knew exactly what a grenade could do. He grabbed the grenade in his mouth and rushed away with it. Minutes later, the grenade exploded. Gander was killed instantly, but he had saved the lives of seven soldiers.

REMEMBERING BRAVERY

After his heroic death, Gander was awarded the Dickin Medal. This is a special medal to honor the work of animals in war. The medal was the idea of Maria Dickin, who spent her life caring for sick animals. It was first awarded in 1943, and it is still given to animal heroes today.

► This is Gander with his regiment in 1941.

Rip the search-and-rescue dog

During World War II, thousands of homes were flattened in bombing raids. Many people were trapped inside fallen buildings. They were often found by search-and-rescue dogs, which looked for survivors in the ruins.

One of these dogs, named Rip, worked in London. After the bombing raids, he walked through the ruined streets with his **handler**. Rip poked his nose into every pile of bricks, checking for signs of life. As soon as he started to dig, a rescue operation began. Rip helped rescue more than 100 people who had been buried alive.

▲ Rip the search-and-rescue dog stands guard over a man he has discovered under a collapsed building.

Commando the messenger pigeon

Commando was one of thousands of messenger pigeons used in World War II. He worked for the British Army, which sent him on missions into France. At the time, France was controlled by Hitler's Nazi government.

Commando was taken into France by **parachute**. He was carried in a special cage and given to a secret agent. The agent used Commando to carry messages back to Britain. Thanks to Commando, the British learned some important secrets about what was happening in France.

NUMBER CRUNCHING

- More than 200,000 pigeons served in World War II.
- Messenger pigeons often flew missions of over 322 kilometers (200 miles) and could reach a speed of 1.6 kilometers (1 mile) a minute.
- Fewer than one in eight messenger pigeons managed to complete their missions successfully.

▼ These pigeons are being trained to carry messages. It was dangerous work. Many were shot down by enemy gunners. Others died from exhaustion or were killed by birds of prey.

ANIMALS IN RECENT WARS

Animals still take part in wars today. Armies all over the world rely on dogs to work as guards. They also use a surprising range of creatures to help them search for **land mines**. These are small but deadly bombs that are buried just below the surface of the ground.

Super sniffers

Some land mines are attached to a **trip wire** that sets off a bomb. Others explode as soon as anyone steps on them.

Armies have trained special sniffer dogs to search for land mines. The dogs use their excellent sense of smell to detect the **explosives** in the buried bomb. Sniffer dogs work with **handlers** and warn them if they smell anything suspicious. Searching for land mines is very dangerous work, but the brave sniffer dogs save countless lives.

▼ Treo worked as a sniffer dog in Afghanistan in 2008. He detected two major land mines.

REMEMBERING BRAVERY

Karl was a U.S. soldier in the Vietnam War (1955–75). He worked as a dog handler with a sniffer dog named Hobo, who saved his life. He was checking out a jungle path with Hobo, when the dog suddenly jumped straight up into the air in warning. Karl came to a stop just in front of a trip wire across the path. Hobo had saved Karl and the 15 men who were following him.

▶ This **memorial** can be seen at Fort Benning, in Georgia. It is to remember all the brave war dogs who have saved soldiers' lives.

Remarkable rats

The problem of buried land mines is especially bad in Africa. More than 12,000 Africans are killed or injured by mines every year.

Some very clever rats have been trained to find land mines in Africa. They have been nicknamed HeroRATs. They are trained to recognize the smell of a mine, and they scratch the ground whenever they find one. The rats are very light, so they do not set off the mines.

NUMBER CRUNCHING

- It takes 8 to 12 months to train a HeroRAT to detect land mines.
- Most HeroRATs work for about four years.
- A HeroRAT takes 30 minutes to scan 100 square meters (1,076 square feet) of land.
- HeroRATs work for about an hour a day.

▼ HeroRATS wear a harness that is controlled from a safe distance. The rat is guided across a patch of ground to make sure it covers every inch.

Dolphin detectives

Bombs can also be planted in the sea. Underwater mines are very hard to find. But some scientists have found a surprising way to deal with them. Scientists in the U.S. Navy train dolphins to search for mines under the sea.

Dolphins are very intelligent creatures, so they soon learn to recognize a mine. When the dolphins find a mine, they drop a floating marker to show its position. Then they swim away into safer waters.

▶ Dolphins have been used to search for mines in the waters around Iraq. This dolphin is wearing a tracking device on its fin.

CONCLUSION

Animals have no choice about their role in war. So, should they ever be sent to battle zones? Some people say it is cruel to put animals in danger. Others think that animals should sometimes be used in war, especially when they help to save people's lives. What do you think?

Caring for animal heroes

Today, most animals working in **war zones** are very well cared for. They have plenty of food and time to rest. **Land mine** detector dogs rarely stay in a war zone for more than a year. During their time on duty, the dogs develop a very close friendship with their **handler**.

▼ Mine detector dogs and their
   handlers work as a team.

Sadly, some animals die in war. However, many enjoy a happy retirement. After a few years of service, most army dogs spend the rest of their lives as much-loved pets.

WHAT WOULD YOU DO?

During World War II, many families offered their pet dogs to be trained for war work. It was a hard decision, but the families knew that their pet could help to save lives. If you had a puppy that was lively, brave, and intelligent, would you be prepared to offer it for war work?

► During World War I, people were told that sending horses to war helped to save soldiers' lives. Many farming families gave their horses to the army to help win the war. Sadly, very few of the horses ever came home again.

Help him to help U.S.!

Help the Horse to Save the Soldier

JAMES MONTGOMERY FLAGG

THE AMERICAN **RED STAR** ANIMAL RELIEF

National Headquarters, Albany, N.Y.

ANIMAL HEROES AROUND THE WORLD

UNITED STATES
The U.S. Army warhorse Comanche was wounded at the Battle of Little Bighorn.

UNITED STATES
Sallie the terrier kept watch over the wounded after the Battle of Gettysburg in the **Civil War**.

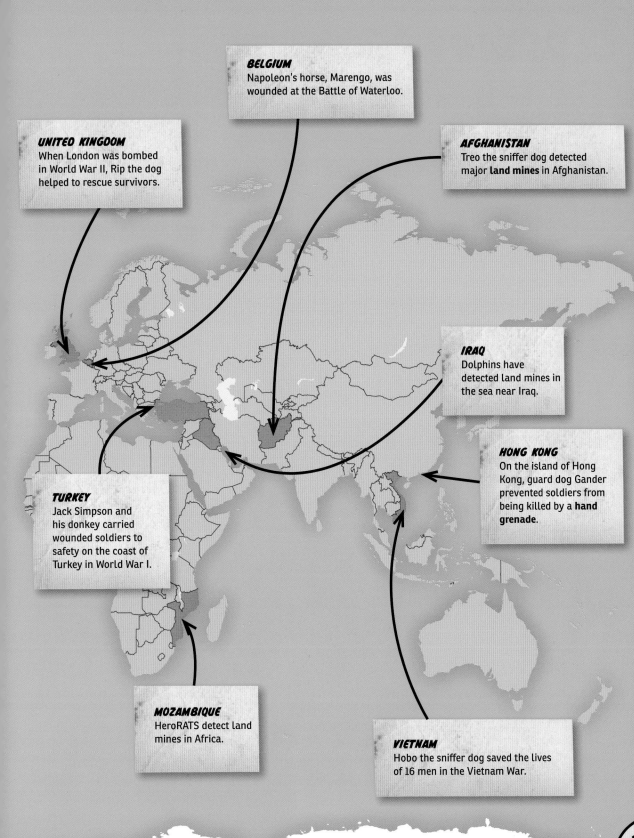

BELGIUM
Napoleon's horse, Marengo, was wounded at the Battle of Waterloo.

UNITED KINGDOM
When London was bombed in World War II, Rip the dog helped to rescue survivors.

AFGHANISTAN
Treo the sniffer dog detected major **land mines** in Afghanistan.

IRAQ
Dolphins have detected land mines in the sea near Iraq.

HONG KONG
On the island of Hong Kong, guard dog Gander prevented soldiers from being killed by a **hand grenade**.

TURKEY
Jack Simpson and his donkey carried wounded soldiers to safety on the coast of Turkey in World War I.

MOZAMBIQUE
HeroRATS detect land mines in Africa.

VIETNAM
Hobo the sniffer dog saved the lives of 16 men in the Vietnam War.

GLOSSARY

aggression deliberate violence or attack

cavalry soldiers who fight on horseback

chariot small, horse-drawn vehicle used in the past for riding into battle

civil war war between different groups of people in the same country

Confederate one of the southern U.S. states that wanted to break away and form their own government in the 1800s

conflict fighting or war

explosive substance, such as gunpowder, that can blow up

hand grenade small bomb that can be thrown by a soldier

handler someone who trains and looks after an animal

land mine small bomb that is buried close to the surface of the ground

mascot something that is supposed to bring good luck

memorial way of remembering the dead

mobile kitchen cooking equipment, such as a stove, that can be moved from place to place

Nazi ruling party of Germany from 1933–45, or a member of it. The Nazis were led by Adolf Hitler.

parachute piece of light cloth attached to people so that, when they jump from a plane, they fall slowly to the ground

poison gas gas used during World War I that killed people and animals by suffocating them

Red Cross international organization that helps people who are wounded in war

regiment group of soldiers who fight together

stretcher-bearer someone who carries injured people on a stretcher

trench long ditches dug into the ground. Soldiers in World War I lived in and fought from trenches.

trip wire wire stretched across a path to make people trip. Some trip wires are attached to land mines.

Union group of northern U.S. states that fought against the southern states that tried to set up their own government in the 1800s

war zone place where a war is being fought

western front large area of northern France and Belgium where most of the fighting took place during World War I

FIND OUT MORE

Books

Nonfiction

Denega, Danielle. *Spy Files: The Cold War Pigeon Patrols and Other Animal Spies*. New York: Franklin Watts, 2008.

George, Isabel, and Rob Lloyd Jones. *Animals at War*. Tulsa, Okla.: EDC, 2007.

Murray, Julie. *Going to Work: Military Animals*. Edina, Minn.: ABDO, 2009.

Fiction

Kadohata, Cynthia. *Cracker!: The Best Dog in Vietnam*. New York: Atheneum, 2008.

Morpurgo, Michael. *War Horse*. New York: Scholastic, 2010.

Websites

www.uswardogs.org
Find out about the animals who have served in the U.S. armed forces in different wars.

www.firstworldwar.com/photos/animals.htm
See pictures of animal heroes from World War I at this multimedia website about World War I.

www.herorat.org
Learn about the training and work of rats that detect land mines in Africa.

A place to visit

The War Dog Memorial
22550 Van Buren Boulevard
Riverside, California 92518

Visit the War Dog Memorial to see how wartime animal heroes are remembered today.

INDEX

Afghanistan 22
American Civil War
  10–11
ancient armies 6
Animals in War
  Memorial, London 5
Australian War
  Memorial 14

badgers 10
Battle of Gettysburg 10
Battle of Little Bighorn
  9
Battle of Waterloo 8
bears 10
birds 4, 10–11, 12,
  16–17, 20–21

camels 5, 7
caring for animal heroes
  26
cats 15
chariots 6
Cher Ami (pigeon)
  16, 17
Comanche (horse) 9
Commando (pigeon) 20
Croix de Guerre 17

Dickin Medal 18
dog handlers 20, 22,
  23, 26
dogs 4, 6, 10, 12, 15,
  18, 20, 22–23, 26, 27
dolphins 5, 25
donkeys 12, 14
Duffy (donkey) 14

eagles 10–11
Egyptians, ancient 6
elephants 5, 6–7

fighting dogs 6

Gander (dog) 18, 19
glowworms 4, 5
guards 22

hand grenades 18
Hannibal 7
HeroRATS 24
Hitler, Adolf 18, 20
Hobo (dog) 23
horses 4, 5, 6, 7, 8, 9,
  12, 13, 27

Joey (horse) 13

land mines 22, 23, 24

Marengo (horse) 8
mascots 10, 18
medals 17, 18
messengers 16, 17,
  20–21
mine detection
  22–25, 26
mines, underwater 25
monuments 5
Morpurgo, Michael 13
mules 12

Napoleon Bonaparte 8

Old Abe (eagle) 10–11

pigeons 4, 12, 16–17,
  20–21
pigs 7
poison gas 13

raccoons 10
rats 24
Red Cross dogs 15
retirement 27
Rip (dog) 20
Romans 6, 7

Sallie (dog) 10
search-and-rescue dogs
  20
Simpson, Jack 14
sniffer dogs 4, 22–23,
  26
spies 16

Treo (dog) 22

Vietnam War 23

War Horse (book and
  play) 13
World War I 4,
  12–17, 27
World War II 18–21, 27